THE LAKE DISTRICT

FROM THE AIR

LAKE STEAMER, WINDERMERE

THE LAKE DISTRICT
FROM THE AIR

Photographs by Aerofilms

LEOPARD

This edition published in 1996 by Leopard,
a division of Random House UK Ltd,
20 Vauxhall Bridge Road, London SW1V 2SA

First published in Great Britain in 1991 by
Barrie & Jenkins

ISBN 0 7529 0422 1

Captions researched and written by Sophia Acland
and Elizabeth Leeming
Map by John Beck

Designed by Carol McCleeve

Typeset by SX Composing Ltd, Rayleigh, Essex
Colour separation by Chroma Graphics, Singapore
Printed and bound in Italy

Photo enlargements
Aerofilms Ltd has an extensive photographic library,
covering the whole of Great Britain. The photos in this
book were selected from several thousand, including
many dating back to 1919. All the photos in the Aerofilms
library are available as photographic enlargements from
the original negative.

Free proofs and price list from:
Aerofilms Limited, Gate Studios, Station Road,
Borehamwood, Herts WD6 1EJ

Please state specifically which locations are of interest

LIST OF AERIAL PHOTOGRAPHS

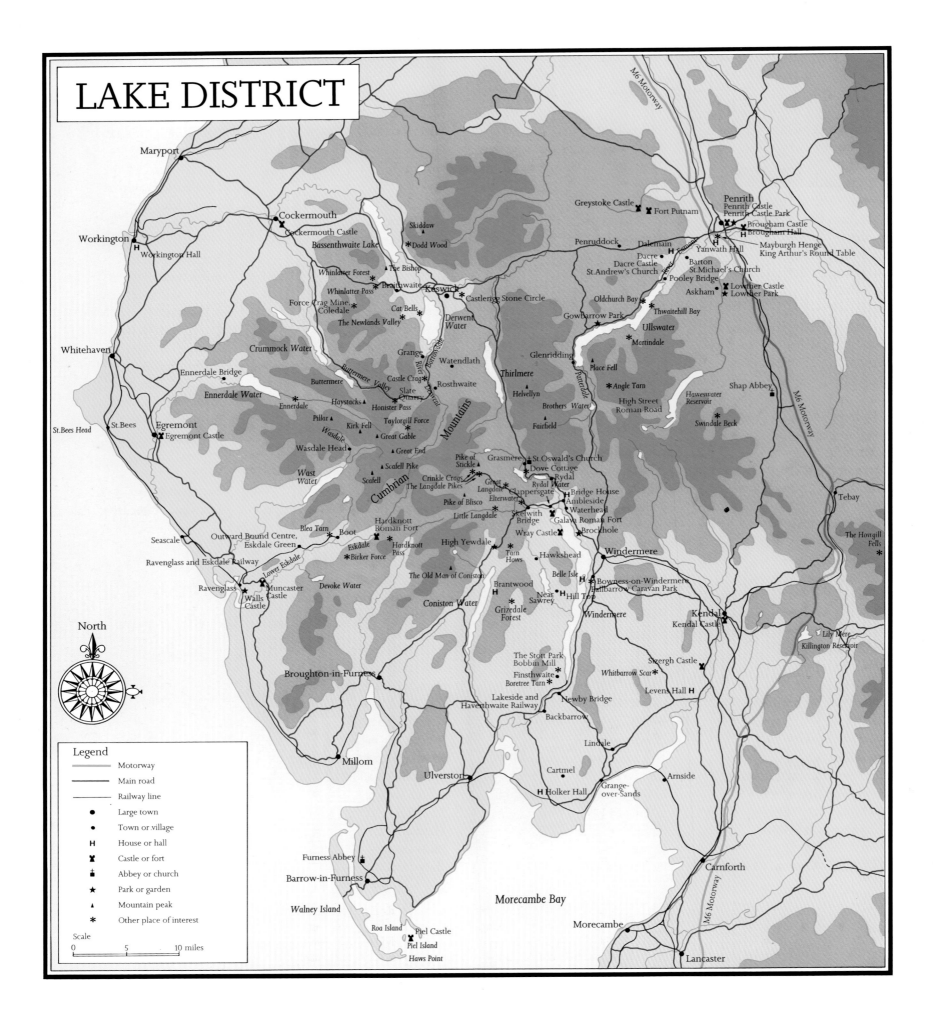

LAKE DISTRICT

Maryport

Workington

Workington Hall H

Cockermouth
Cockermouth Castle

Bassenthwaite Lake

Skiddaw
Dodd Wood

Greystoke Castle
Fort Putnam

Penrith
Penrith Castle
Penrith Castle Park
Brougham Castle
Brougham Hall

Penruddock
Dalemain
Mayburgh Henge
King Arthur's Round Table

Dacre
Dacre Castle
St.Andrew's Church

Yanwath Hall
Barton
St.Michael's Church

Whinlatter Forest
The Bishop

Whinlatter Pass
Braithwaite
Keswick

Force Crag Mine,
Coledale
Cat Bells

Castlerigg Stone Circle

Oldchurch Bay

Pooley Bridge
Lowther Castle
Askham
Lowther Park

The Newlands Valley

Derwent
Water

Gowbarrow Park
Thwaitehill Bay
Ullswater

Whitehaven

Crummock Water

Grange
Watendlath

Glenridding

Martindale

Ennerdale Bridge

Buttermere Valley
Castle Crag
Rosthwaite

Thirlmere
Helvellyn

Place Fell

Angle Tarn

Shap Abbey

St.Bees Head

Ennerdale Water

Buttermere
Haystacks
Honister Pass
Slate
Quarry

Brothers Water
Fairfield

High Street
Roman Road

Haweswater
Reservoir

Swindale Beck

St.Bees
Egremont
Egremont Castle

Ennerdale

Pillar
Kirk Fell
Wasdale

Taylorgill Force
Great Gable

Cumbrian
Mountains

Great End

Wasdale Head

Scafell Pike

Pike of
Stickle

Grasmere
St.Oswald's Church
Dove Cottage
Rydal
Rydal Water

Wast
Water

Scafell

Crinkle Crags
The Langdale Pikes

Great
Langdale

Elterwater

Bridge House
Ambleside
Waterhead

Pike of Blisco
Little Langdale

Clappersgate

Skelwith
Bridge

Galava Roman Fort

The Howgill
Fells

Tebay

Blea Tarn
Boot

Hardknott
Roman Fort

High Yewdale

Wray Castle
Brockhole

Seascale

Outward Bound Centre,
Eskdale Green

Eskdale
Hardknott
Pass

Tarn
Hows

Hawkshead

Windermere

Ravenglass and Eskdale Railway

Birker Force

The Old Man of Coniston

Belle Isle

Bowness-on-Windermere
Hawbarrow Caravan Park

Ravenglass
Walls
Castle
Muncaster
Castle

Devoke Water

Brantwood
Near
Sawrey
Hill Top

Windermere

Kendal
Kendal Castle

Lily Mere
Killington Reservoir

Coniston Water

Grizedale
Forest

Broughton-in-Furness

The Stott Park
Bobbin Mill
Finsthwaite
Boretree Tarn

Sizergh Castle

Whitbarrow Scar

Levens Hall

Legend

	Motorway
	Main road
	Railway line
●	Large town
•	Town or village
H	House or hall
✗	Castle or fort
♦	Abbey or church
★	Park or garden
▲	Mountain peak
✳	Other place of interest

Lakeside and
Haverthwaite Railway

Newby Bridge

Backbarrow

Millom

Lindale

Ulverston

Cartmel

Arnside

Scale

0   5   10 miles

North

Furness Abbey

Holker Hall

Grange-
over-Sands

Carnforth

Barrow-in-Furness

Walney Island

Roa Island
Piel Castle
Piel Island
Haws Point

Morecambe Bay

Morecambe

Lancaster

GREYSTOKE CASTLE

The barony of Greystoke is an ancient one, and parts of the existing castle are
thought to date from the twelfth century. However, like so many medieval castles it
suffered grievously in the Civil War, when it was largely destroyed by fire.
Rebuilt in c. 1675 and enlarged in 1789, it owes its present neo-Elizabethan
appearance to the architect Anthony Salvin who remodelled it in 1868.

FORT PUTNAM, GREYSTOKE

This extraordinary building is not, as one might be tempted to think, a bizarre
variation on the familiar Lake District theme of fortifying one's home to keep out the
marauding Scots. Instead it owes its existence to a whim of the 11th Duke of
Norfolk, owner of the Greystoke estate, who in the late eighteenth century built this
and two other fantastic folly farms just to the east of Greystoke Castle.

PENRITH

Penrith's street plan still reflects its turbulent medieval past: the streets are
narrow with open spaces – like Great Dockray to the right of the first picture – into
which animals could be herded when Scottish raids threatened. Nowadays, more
prosaically, many form handy car parks. In the centre and left of the picture is Corn
Market. Penrith was granted a market charter in 1223 and the modern market is held here.

When Celia Fiennes visited Penrith in 1698 the predominantly red colour of
the buildings made her think at first they were made of brick but in fact, then as
today, the characteristic warm colour came from the local red sandstone.
Shown here is the town centre with the Victorian Musgrave monument in the market
place and, to the right, the medieval tower of the parish church of St Andrew.

PENRITH CASTLE PARK

The neat symmetry and contrasting colours of the circular garden in the middle
of Penrith's Castle Park make a pleasing composition for the aerial photographer on a
sunny day. This is Penrith's main leisure area, with tennis courts, bowls, mini
golf, a children's play area and, of course, the castle ruins to explore. Behind the
central summer house can be seen Penrith's war memorial, known as the Black Angel.

PENRITH CASTLE

Penrith Castle stands rather forlorn today, part of its moat sliced off in an
undignified manner by the modern road to the railway station. It is thought to have
been built in the late fourteenth century by William Strickland (who later
became Bishop of Carlisle) to protect the town against the Scots, and was added to by
Richard, Duke of Gloucester, the future Richard III.

BROUGHAM CASTLE

Brougham, the most impressive of the Lake District's ruined castles, lies in a
peaceful setting beside the River Eamont. The keep dates to c. 1176; the curtain wall
and gatehouses were added around the turn of the thirteenth century and the
whole was restored in 1651-62. This site has been fortified for even longer: the
Romans built their fort of Brocavum just to the south of the present castle.

BROUGHAM HALL RUINS

In its heyday in the nineteenth century Brougham Hall, home of the Lord
Chancellor of the same name, was known as 'the Windsor of the North', a frequent
stopping point for the royal family on their journeys to Scotland. Built between
1830 and 1840, the great house was pulled down in 1934, but it has lately become
the subject of an ambitious restoration programme, housing numerous small businesses.

MAYBURGH HENGE

At Eamont Bridge, just south of Penrith, are two remarkable Neolithic
monuments. Incongruously situated beside the M6 is Mayburgh Henge, which has
massive banks of gathered stone rubble surrounding a single 15-foot standing
stone. Until the eighteenth century there were seven other such stones but these seem
sadly to have been removed as a convenient source of building stone.

KING ARTHUR'S ROUND TABLE

Just two or three hundred yards away from Mayburgh is a second henge, with
the rather more fanciful name of King Arthur's Round Table. Since, like its neighbour,
it is actually thought to date from c. 2000 BC, it rather predates this legendary
hero. Unlike Mayburgh, this henge was built by digging a ditch and embanking the
spoil; both henges are thought to have been temples.

DALEMAIN

Behind the elegant Georgian facade of Dalemain near Pooley Bridge is a
fascinating interior comprising a twelfth-century pele tower and a rabbit warren of
Tudor rooms as well as the fine Georgian section, added in 1745. Some of the
deer from Dalemain's deer park can be seen above the house; visitors are also lured by
excellent meals in the medieval Old Hall.

BARTON

Barton's lovely church is not, as one might expect, the focal point of a busy
village. The name 'Barton' in fact refers to buildings belonging to an arable farm and
the church's only neighbours have always been farms and a vicarage. Church
Farm, to the left, built in 1637, was the first vicarage; its Victorian successor can be
seen nearer the church. Between them is another farm, Glebe Farm.

ST MICHAEL'S CHURCH, BARTON

Surprisingly large for its isolated location, the fine Norman church of St
Michael's, Barton, stands on a mound in a circular churchyard that may have been
used as a pre-Christian place of worship. Founded in c. 1150 and extended in
1330, it once served a vast parish stretching from Eamont Bridge to Patterdale.
Wordsworth's grandfather is buried in the chancel.

YANWATH HALL

Yanwath, with its squat, stout pele tower, neat garden and attractive adjoining
courtyard of farm buildings, presents a charming picture of domestic order when seen
from above, and has been described as the best example of a manorial hall in
England. The beautifully preserved tower and range of buildings alongside were built
by John de Sutton in 1322; the courtyard buildings were added in the fifteenth century.

RIVER EAMONT, ULLSWATER

*As Ullswater snakes its way north-eastwards it leaves the grand volcanic fells
that surround its southern end and crosses gentler terrain before the River Eamont,
emerging at its northern end, reaches a belt of carboniferous limestone and the
peaceful green pastures associated with it. From here the Eamont plots a wayward
course north-eastwards towards Penrith and on to its confluence with the Eden.*

PENRUDDOCK AND THE NORTHERN FELLS

From above, the Lake District's most northerly group of fells seems to rear up
like an island from a green sea of agricultural land. Composed of one of the oldest
rocks on Earth, Skiddaw slate, which formed about 500 million years ago,
these fells are dominated by Blencathra, or Saddleback, on the left, and Skiddaw,
behind. This view is taken from the east, with Penruddock in the foreground.

LOWTHER CASTLE

There has been a house on the site of this spectacular ruin since the days of
Edward I, but most of the traces of earlier structures were wiped out by a disastrous
fire in 1717. The present extraordinary mansion with its plethora of towers and
spires was built by Robert Smirke (later architect of the British Museum) for the
second Earl of Lonsdale in 1806-10.

LOWTHER CASTLE

In 1956 the roof of Lowther Castle was removed and the house abandoned –
one can imagine that it was hardly an economical place to maintain. The result,
though, is particularly striking when seen from above – the massive grey walls
and sightless windows looking out on the steadily encroaching armies of conifers give
the house a decidedly sinister air, even on a sunny day. Lowther's curious
mixture of Gothic and baronial style architecture has not always aroused unalloyed
praise but one Lakeland neighbour was in no doubt about its merits:
Wordsworth wrote of it
'Lowther! In thy majestic pile are seen
Cathedral pomp and grace, in apt accord
With the baronial castle's sterner mien . . .'

LOWTHER PARK

*Seen here from the north, Lowther Castle is set in magnificent rolling parkland
beside the River Lowther, crossed by two fine avenues of oak trees. The well-known
Lowther Horse Driving Trials and Country Fair are held here each August; in
the South Park, in the distance to the left, is the Lowther Leisure Park, a family
entertainment centre.*

ASKHAM

Set in gentle limestone scenery, the village of Askham is one of the prettiest in
the Lake District. It straggles attractively up a slope from the River Lowther, divided for
almost its entire length by an extended 'village green'. Askham Hall, based on
a fourteenth-century tower, can be seen to the right; it has been the home of the Earl
of Lonsdale since nearby Lowther Castle was abandoned.

DACRE CASTLE

Based on an early fourteenth-century pele tower, Dacre's castle, south-west of
Penrith, has changed less from its original forbidding appearance than have other Lake
District houses such as Sizergh or Levens. For many years a seat of the Dacre
family, it passed to Edward Hasell of nearby Dalemain in 1723 and is still part of the
Dalemain Estate. It was restored to its present state in 1963.

ST ANDREW'S CHURCH, DACRE

Dacre's fine Norman parish church, restored in Victorian times, almost
certainly stands on the site of an even more interesting piece of ecclesiastical history –
an eighth-century monastery mentioned by the Venerable Bede. The
archaeological dig to try to confirm this, shown here, has since finished and a number
of Anglo-Saxon artefacts were found.

ULLSWATER

*This is Ullswater's tranquil eastern shore, warmed by the sun. The bay on the
left is Howtown Wyke; the fells standing guard behind are Steel End on the left, The
Nab beyond, and Hallin Fell, crowned by an obelisk, on the right. A pleasant
lakeside walk skirts the base of this small but steep-sided hill and a scramble to the
summit is rewarded by a lovely view of the lake.*

GOWBARROW PARK, ULLSWATER

In April 1802, William Wordsworth and his sister Dorothy went on an
expedition to Gowbarrow on the shores of Ullswater and it was in the woods below
the park that they saw the 'golden daffodils' later immortalised in
Wordsworth's poem. Dorothy recorded the scene in her journal: 'I never saw daffodils
so beautiful. They . . . tossed & reeled & danced & seemed as if they verily
laughed with the wind . . .'

CASTLERIGG STONE CIRCLE

The Lake District has several impressive stone circles but Castlerigg, on a hill
east of Keswick in the shadow of Skiddaw and Blencathra, has the most spectacular
site. Late Neolithic or early Bronze Age in date, Castlerigg's purpose is
unknown although theories are legion; eighteenth-century antiquarians thought it was
a druids' circle and more recently it has been variously described as a meeting
place for commerce, a calendar and a place of worship.

POOLEY BRIDGE

*The little village of Pooley Bridge, not far from Penrith, straddles the gentle
River Eamont at the point where it leaves Ullswater. There is an ancient fort whose
outline can still be traced on the wooded hill to the left, but most people come
here nowadays to catch one of the Ullswater lake steamers which sail between here
and Glenridding to the south.*

OLDCHURCH BAY, ULLSWATER

Seen here on a still, misty morning, Ullswater is a lake of many moods.
Second only to Windermere in size, it is in many ways the more interesting of the two
with its combination of sinuous shape, quiet waters and superbly varied
surrounding terrain. To Wordsworth it seemed to have 'the happiest combination of
beauty and grandeur which any of the Lakes affords'.

THWAITEHILL BAY, ULLSWATER

*A group of gleaming white-painted sailing boats moored in Thwaitehill Bay on
Ullswater's eastern shore makes a delightful, almost abstract picture when seen from
above. Neighbouring Sharrow Bay is the base for the Ullswater Yacht Club;
since Ullswater is the Lake District's second longest lake and yet has a speed limit
which outlaws fast motorboats and waterskiers, it is ideal for sailing.*

SEA PLANE, WINDERMERE

Exuding a certain sense of superiority as it is admired by circling motorboats is
a little seaplane, moored in one of Windermere's many sheltered inlets. This is a
Sunderland Flying Boat, which spent two weeks on the lake during the
Windermere Festival in July. These seaplanes were built during the war at Whitecross
Bay; this is the last one still flying.

LAKE STEAMER RAVEN, ULLSWATER

Two charming Victorian steamers still operate a regular service from April to
October along the length of Ullswater. The Raven, shown here, was launched in
1889, and her sister ship, Lady of the Lake, in 1877; both now run on
diesel rather than steam power. Based at Glenridding, they sail to Howtown on the
eastern shore and on to Pooley Bridge in the north.

GLENRIDDING

The northern side of the Glenridding valley, near Ullswater, bears intriguing scars from
its industrial past. Lead was first mined here in the mid-eighteenth century; and in the nineteenth
century, under the auspices of the Greenside Mining Company, the industry
boomed, with shares in the company increasing tenfold in 1827-37 and sophisticated
electric winding gear being installed towards 1900. The mine was abandoned in 1962.

HELVELLYN

The most frequently climbed mountain in the Lake District, Helvellyn is also its
third highest, at 3118 ft. It presents very different appearances from different sides –
from the east, as shown here, the approach is by the dramatic knife-edged
ridges of Striding Edge (in the centre of the picture) or Swirral Edge (to the right). The
flat, grassy summit comes as a welcome reward – it is so flat than an
aeroplane landed successfully here in 1926.

The summit of Helvellyn is the highest point in the great ridge of fells – from
Dollywaggon Pike in the south to Great Dodd six miles away – that divides the valleys
of Thirlmere and Ullswater. Striding Edge is Helvellyn's most dramatic feature,
and in the past enjoyed a fearsome reputation among walkers and climbers, but if
treated with care this 'most exciting of all walkers' routes' as Wainwright calls
it, is mostly an easy scramble. Beyond Striding Edge can be seen Red Tarn and to its
left, in the middle distance, the summit of Catstycam. In the distance to the
right is Ullswater.

PLACE FELL

The fells surrounding Ullswater provide some of the best easy walking in
Lakeland. Shown here is the 2,135-foot summit of Place Fell, which overlooks the
south-eastern corner of the lake. A climb to the summit here can be combined
with a return route amongst woodland and open country beside Ullswater, and there
are fine views for much of the way.

PATTERDALE AND BROTHERS WATER

South of Ullswater is the narrow valley of Patterdale. Its flat alluvial floor
suggests that little Brothers Water, in the distance, was once joined to its larger
neighbour as part of one long lake. Brothers Water gets its name from two
unlucky pairs of brothers who drowned here. To the right is curving Deepdale; beyond
Brothers Water the road rises steeply over the Kirkstone Pass.

MARTINDALE

Remote Martindale, south of Ullswater, is reached by road only via a steep
'hause' or pass from Howtown. Although it consists of just a few scattered farms and
houses on the valley floor, it has two churches, seventeenth-century St Martin's
and nineteenth-century St Peter's. The valley on the right of the picture is Boredale; to
the left is Howe Grain.

SWINDALE BECK

The steep-sided valley drained by Swindale Beck must be one of the most
secretively beautiful and least frequented in the Lake District. It lies in the east of the
area, amidst the little-visited fells between Haweswater and Shap, and the beck
falls to the north-east into the River Lowther. At the head of the dale a visit to the fine
series of waterfalls is well worth the walk.

ANGLE TARN

This pretty tarn's distinctive shape makes it easily recognisable. It lies south-
east of Patterdale and, looking north, one can see Angletarn Pikes and Heck Crag
beyond, with the valleys of Boredale and Bannerdale to left and right. High Street crosses
Loadpot Hill on the ridge to the right and in the distance stretches Ullswater with
the Eden Valley beyond and – just discernible – the buildings of Penrith.

HIGH STREET ROMAN ROAD

Between their forts of Brocavum (Brougham) and Galava (Ambleside), the
Romans built the remarkable road known as High Street, the highest Roman road in
England, probably using an existing British route. It seems the legionaries felt
safer from ambush by warlike Celtic tribesmen if they kept to the fell tops. High Street
fell, shown here, takes its name from the road, still used as a footpath.

HAWESWATER RESERVOIR

*Compared with neighbouring natural lakes, the bleached, barren shoreline of
Haweswater, caused by fluctuations in the water level, is unsightly, although the
patterns made when the water is low are intriguing. The reservoir, which
supplies industrial Lancashire, was formed in the late 1930s by raising the level of an
existing lake by 96 feet; sadly, in the process the pretty village of Mardale was drowned.*

M6 MOTORWAY, TEBAY

*After the extravagant man-made loops of interchange 38 at Tebay, the M6
motorway settles down to follow an ancient route southwards. This is the Lune Gap,
where road, river and railway together pass between the Howgills to the left,
and Bretherdale, Roundthwaite and Whinfell Commons to the right. This stretch of
motorway has been described as the most scenic in the country.*

GALAVA ROMAN FORT

At Waterhead near Ambleside are the remains of a Roman fort dating to AD
100-120. The Romans first entered the Lake District to subdue the warlike native
Brigantes in c. AD 80; they built an earth and timber fort here but later rebuilt
it in stone. The central rectangle comprised, from left to right, the commandant's
house, the principia or main administrative building, and the granary.

SHAP ABBEY

When the Premonstratensian abbey at Shap, high in the eastern fells, was
dissolved in 1540, some of its buildings were converted into a farm, which still exists
today, hence the rather incongruous juxtaposition of old and new in this picture. The
abbey, on the banks of the River Lowther, was founded around 1200, although the
beautiful west tower of its church, which still stands almost to full height, dates to c. 1500.

ST OSWALD'S CHURCH, GRASMERE

Described by Wordsworth as a building of 'rude and antique majesty', St
Oswald's dates in its oldest part from the thirteenth century. The poet chose its
churchyard as his final resting place, and his grave lies beneath the shade of
one of the yews he planted himself. St Oswald's is the scene every summer of the
colourful Rushbearing Festival, a long-lived northern tradition.

GRASMERE

The village of Grasmere, set amidst emerald fields beside its own small lake, is
one of the most visited in the Lakes. Its attractions include the popular traditional
Grasmere Sports, held in August, the famous gingerbread, the glorious
surrounding scenery and, of course, its literary connections: this is the heart of
Wordsworth country. The poet lived in no less than four different houses in the
Grasmere area and described the place as 'the loveliest spot that man hath ever found'.

GRASMERE ISLAND

The sunlight catching the ripples on the water surrounding little Grasmere
Island makes a glorious picture for the aerial photographer. The Lakes have long been
one of the most painted and photographed parts of the British Isles, from the
seventeenth-century engravers who accompanied the area's first 'tourists', to the
paintings of Turner, Constable and their successors and, in the present century,
photographers such as the Abrahams of Keswick, Joseph Hardman and Geoffrey Berry.

RYDAL WATER AND GRASMERE

*Sharing Grasmere's valley, just a short way downstream along the River
Rothay, is a second small glacial lake, Rydal Water. On both, glacial deposits known
as drumlins have formed small islands, and they share, too, the same lovely
gently rolling wooded landscape, so different from the extravagant drama of the high
volcanic fells to the west (which can be seen in the distance).*

DOVE COTTAGE, GRASMERE

Home to William Wordsworth from 1799–1808, this modest white cottage
(seen to the left of the minor road with the museum behind), is now an important and
popular shrine to the poet. Wordsworth enjoyed a 'Golden Decade' at Dove
Cottage, producing much of his best-known work, and it was here his sister Dorothy
recorded the family's everyday experiences in her poetic journals.

FAIRFIELD

The broad and grassy summit of Fairfield (2863 feet) is the goal of one of the
most popular 'round' walks in Lakeland, the Fairfield Horseshoe. The most common
ascent is from Rydal, to the south, but the route from Patterdale brings one up
from St Sunday Crag along the ridge to the right of the picture, and gives a view of the
splendid crags of the north face as seen here.

GREAT LANGDALE

Great Langdale is a narrow, sparsely populated valley – that is except for the
armies of walkers who make their way here every summer to tackle the surrounding
fells: the famous Langdale Pikes and Bowfell (both out of sight to the right),
Crinkle Crags (which crown the Oxendale valley straight ahead) and Pike of Blisco (to
the left of Crinkle Crags).

ELTERWATER

The sinuous curves of the smallest of the sixteen Lake District lakes are seen to
excellent effect from above. Elterwater lies at the bottom of the valleys of Great and
Little Langdale, west of Ambleside. Only half a mile long, it is steadily silting
up and becoming still smaller. Its reedy shores are a haven for wildfowl, as befits its
name, which means 'swan lake' in Norse.

WRAY CASTLE

It was in Wray Castle (just visible in the bottom right hand corner of picture)
that Beatrix Potter spent the first of those Lake District holidays that were to inspire
her children's books. Built in the 1840's, the castle takes the form of an
extravagant medieval fortress. One can well imagine the impression made on the
young girl by this backdrop of the greatest fells in Lakeland.

LITTLE LANGDALE

*Little Langdale, here seen in glowing autumn colours, is a delectable valley
with its own small tarn. A road between Wrynose Fell and Lingmoor Fell on its far
side passes Blea Tarn (just visible in the centre of the picture) on its way to
neighbouring Great Langdale. In the distance, to the right, rises the unmistakable
rugged profile of the Langdale Pikes.*

SKELWITH BRIDGE

*Just downstream from Elterwater at Skelwith Bridge, the River Brathay tumbles
over the boulders of Skelwith Force – the white water can be seen to the left of the
village. The waterfall is only 20 feet high but since the Brathay carries the
water draining from both Great and Little Langdale into Elterwater, the volume of
water falling is the greatest in the Lake District.*

CLAPPERSGATE

Along the banks of the River Brathay east of Skelwith Bridge lies the small
village of Clappersgate. The large white house was built by a prosperous Liverpool
merchant in the eighteenth century, later becoming the Croft Hotel and now
converted into flats. The boat house and harbour of Croft Lodge were once a wharf for
the loading of slate – which gave Clappersgate the status of a port.

TARN HOWS

One of the Lake District's most famous beauty spots, Tarn Hows was created
from three smaller tarns at the turn of the century. In 1930 the owner Sir Samuel
Scott gave it to the National Trust which struggles to cope with the hordes of
visitors who come to admire the larch and spruce woodlands, the two pretty islands
and the magnificent backdrop of rolling fells.

WATERHEAD AND AMBLESIDE

*Ambleside and its lakeshore offshoot, Waterhead, command a spectacular
position at the head of Windermere, backed on three sides by high fells. Its surroundings,
and the town's reputation as a good 'kitting-out' centre for fell-walkers, attract visitors
like a magnet and clog the one-way system with impatient motorists in the summer.
The pier in the foreground is the terminus at Waterhead for the ferry.*

BRIDGE HOUSE, AMBLESIDE

Lilliputian Bridge House, just two rooms connected by an outside staircase,
dates from the sixteenth century and is said to have been built as a summer house and
apple store by the Braithwaite family of the old Ambleside Hall. Owned by the
National Trust, it is used as an information centre during the summer months. Stock
Ghyll, which flows beneath this unusual bridge, once powered several mills.

HAWKSHEAD

In 'The Prelude' Wordsworth describes this small market town where he spent
his school-days (the grammar school, now a museum and library, is the modest white
house nearest to view). Hawkshead was once within the lands of Furness Abbey
and prospered as a 'wool town'. Visitors' vehicles are prohibited in the centre – an
attempt to preserve the picturesque hodge-podge of tiny squares and cobbled lanes.

LAKE DISTRICT NATIONAL PARK CENTRE, BROCKHOLE

Once the home of an enlightened Manchester cotton magnate, this elegant late-
nineteenth century mansion on the shores of Windermere is now the headquarters of
the National Park and an excellent visitor centre. Both the serious student and
the holiday-maker can appreciate what Brockhole has to offer. Its landscaped garden
which slopes down to the lake has a fine collection of mature trees.

BRANTWOOD

The personality of John Ruskin still pervades his cherished home. The
prodigiously talented Victorian poet, artist, critic and social revolutionary bought
Brantwood, with its magnificent views across Coniston, in 1871 and lived there
from 1872 until his death in 1900. He embellished and improved the house and filled
it with priceless treasures. Preserved as a national memorial, it is open to the public.

HILL TOP, NEAR SAWREY

Beatrix Potter bought this seventeenth-century Westmorland farmhouse in 1905
with the income from her Peter Rabbit books. Seven of the books
were set in the village and farm, and visitors find there enchanting reminders of familiar scenes and
characters. This dedicated countrywoman left her home to the National Trust to be
preserved unchanged, an example of her deep concern about the conservation of the Lake District.

WINDERMERE

Blue and serene, surrounded by gently sloping wooded inlets, it is easy to see
why Windermere has attracted countless visitors since the eighteenth century. Its size –
at nearly 11 miles it is England's longest lake – has made it a recreational lake par excellence,
and today it is constantly busy with boat traffic of all kinds.
The picture is taken looking north, with Lakeside in the foreground on the left-hand side.

BOWNESS-ON-WINDERMERE

On Lake Windermere's eastern shore, Bowness is the busiest of all the Lake
District's holiday resorts. It is an old town, founded in the tenth century by Norse
settlers, one of whom also gave his name to the lake: 'Vinand's Mere' or
Windermere. It expanded to its present size after the coming of the railway to the
hamlet of Birthwaite, just to the north, in 1847.

FALLBARROW CARAVAN PARK, BOWNESS-ON-WINDERMERE

Every taste in holiday accommodation is catered for in the Lake District – from
such august eateries as the Sharrow Bay and Miller Howe hotels to countless lesser
inns, guest houses and farmhouses offering bed and breakfast, self-catering
cottages and, of course, caravan parks. The Fallbarrow Park, shown here, has an
enviable location beside Windermere and good facilities.

BELLE ISLE, WINDERMERE

On Windermere's largest island, Belle Isle, just opposite Bowness, stands a
remarkable testament to the eighteenth-century quest for aestheticism: England's
earliest completely round house. It was built in 1774 for a wealthy
Nottingham merchant, Thomas English. Ridiculed by the locals, he lost heart in the
project and sold it in 1781 to the Curwen family who still own it.

GRIZEDALE FOREST

Lush Grizedale Forest is the largest Forestry Commission plantation in the Lake
District. The Commission, founded in 1919, earned much local opposition in its early
years by planting ugly lines of conifers; here instead it aimed to provide
woodland that was also a recreational area. The result is a beautiful forest with
marked walks, photographic hides and an excellent Forest Visitor and Wildlife Centre.

WINDERMERE

A dusting of snow on the slopes of Wansfell Pike above Ambleside and the sun
catching its reflection in the seemingly endless waters of Lake Windermere make a
stunning composition for the bird's eye photographer. To the right of the lake
can be seen Blelham Tarn and, beyond it, Esthwaite Water; in the distance to the far
right is Coniston Water.

BORETREE TARN

On the gently sloping higher ground west of Lake Windermere is a series of
small, pretty tarns set in mixed woodland. Cross-shaped Boretree Tarn, the most
southerly of them, makes an attractive picture from the air on an autumn
evening. A glimpse of neighbouring High Dam can be seen above it to the left, and
beyond is the southern end of Windermere, overlooked by Gummer's How.

KENDAL CASTLE

On a low glacial hill on the east side of the River Kent stands one of Kendal's
two castles. This one's main claim to fame is as the birthplace of Henry VIII's sixth
and final wife, Katherine Parr, but it fell into decay after her brother died
without heirs in 1571. On the opposite bank of the river is Castle Howe, site of an
earlier castle built around 1092.

KENDAL

Stretching out on both sides of the River Kent for more than two miles, Kendal,
home of the famous Mint Cake, is an attractive old town whose market charter dates
from 1189. In the foreground on the left bank of the river can be seen two of its
best-known buildings: the thirteenth-century Church of the Holy Trinity which, with
its five aisles, is one of the largest parish churches in England. Next to it is
Abbot Hall, built by John Carr of York in 1759, which houses the well known art
gallery of the same name and, in the stable block, the Museum of Lakeland
Life and Industry.

Built mainly of local limestone with slate roofs, Kendal, the 'Auld Grey Town',
thoroughly lives up to its nickname in this view. The narrow streets of older houses
opening into hidden yards are a reminder of the days when the town's
inhabitants had to be constantly on their guard against Scottish raiders. Shown here is
part of the town centre with the baroque Town Hall, which dates to 1825, at
centre left, and at top right, the new Westmorland Shopping Centre.

WHITBARROW SCAR

Whitbarrow Scar is a great slab of carboniferous limestone (rare in the
National Park) to the north-east of Witherslack – a dream for the naturalist as it is a
perfect environment for rare flora, fauna and birds. Public footpaths with
magnificent views provide easy routes across the scar although climbing areas are
limited and there is a closed season to allow birds to breed in peace.

KILLINGTON RESERVOIR AND LILY MERE

As motorway service stations go, Killington, on the M6 east of Kendal, must
surely be one of the more agreeable, situated as it is on the shores of peaceful
Killington Reservoir with the Howgill fells rolling away to the north east as a
spectacular backdrop. The reservoir was constructed in 1819 as a feeder for the Kendal-
Lancaster canal; at the time it was the largest canal reservoir in the country.

THE HOWGILL FELLS

*We have crossed over into the north-west corner of the Yorkshire Dales
National Park in order to include the springy, rolling Howgill Fells, the delight of
walkers and naturalists, their rounded profile honed from ancient Silurian
slates. In the shadow to the left is the waterfall, Cautley Spout, flanked by Cautley
Crag and Yarlside. The flat area beyond the fells is the beautiful Eden Valley.*

SIZERGH CASTLE

Sizergh is one of the Lake District's finest fortified houses, based on a 58-foot
high pele tower dating to c. 1340. Pele towers, which provided a refuge from the
Scottish raids of the fourteenth century, are common in Cumbria but Sizergh's
is one of the largest. The Great Hall was added in 1450 and later remodelling
produced a predominantly Elizabethan country house of great charm.

LEVENS HALL

Levens, five miles south of Kendal, is one of Cumbria's largest Elizabethan
houses. It incorporates a fourteenth-century pele tower and a medieval hall but its
chief glory is the famous topiary garden, the best of its kind in the world, laid
out by Monsieur Beaumont, gardener to Charles II and James II, in 1692. The trees
are yew and beech, and are bordered by box.

BACKBARROW

Sandwiched between the Lakeside and Haverthwaite Railway and the A590 is
what was once an important centre of industry. The Backbarrow iron furnace, founded
in 1738, used much of the charcoal produced in the Furness fells and the Blue
Works, established in 1890, manufactured blue for industrial purposes until 1981.
The mill that housed the Blue Works is now a time-share leisure complex.

FINSTHWAITE AND THE STOTT PARK BOBBIN MILL

Finsthwaite lies a mile to the north-west of Lakeside at the southern end of
Windermere. Its late-nineteenth century church replaced an earlier structure, and
Jacobites visit the burial ground to see the grave of the 'Finsthwaite Princess',
Clementa Johannes Sobieska Douglas, said by some to be an illegitimate daughter of
the Young Pretender. Finsthwaite's major attraction, however, is English
Heritage's Stott Park Bobbin Mill. Open for business and owned by the Coward family
from 1835-1971 it is maintained as a working monument; to browse there is
to enjoy a glimpse of nineteenth century rural industry. The bobbin industry grew with
the cotton trade, and the Lake District was responsible for an estimated half of
total output. While some mills turned to steam, Stott Park relied throughout most of
its existence on water from Dam Tarn on Finsthwaite Heights, first using
conventional wheels and later, turbines.

NEWBY BRIDGE

This handsome bridge that spans the River Leven gives the nearby village its
name. In 1651 the existing timber bridge was considered by local notables to require
replacement, and the present five-arched stone structure was built. The River
Leven meanders through woods and meadows from Windermere to its estuary below
Greenodd; just below the bridge is a weir which controls the level of the lake.

LAKESIDE AND HAVERTHWAITE RAILWAY

Shorter than its Eskdale counterpart, 'La'al Ratty', this railway nevertheless
provides an equally popular outing for visitors. In the nineteenth century one could
travel on this standard gauge line from Manchester to Ambleside, with steamer
connections at either end. Today's four-mile journey through the beautiful Leven
Valley to Lakeside Pier recaptures something of the spirit of those Victorian times.

LINDALE

The iron-master John 'iron-mad' Wilkinson (1728-1808) was brought up in,
and retired to, this small village at the foot of Newton Fell. He is remembered by a
forty-foot high cast-iron obelisk – intended, at his request, to mark his grave,
but now standing in the centre of the village; his cast-iron coffin was, like the
memorial, made to his own design.

CARTMEL

The enchanting village of Cartmel boasts the unusual combination of the
magnificent remains of an Augustinian Priory and the smallest National Hunt
racecourse in the country. The priory, founded in 1188 by the 1st Earl of Pembroke,
suffered violent treatment at the Dissolution but the church survived for use by the parish,
and the gatehouse still spans a pretty row of cottages in the village square.

HOLKER HALL

On sheltered, low-lying land jutting out into Morecambe Bay, the garden at Holker Hall has
recently earned the accolade of 'world class' from The Good Gardens Guide.
There are 23 acres of formal and woodland gardens including glorious rhododendrons
and azaleas as can be seen here. The house dates to the early sixteenth century;
a Victorian wing, which is open to the public, was added in 1874.

ULVERSTON

In the north-east of the Furness Peninsula, Ulverston is a fine old market town
with curving narrow streets, an ancient church, and two other fringe attractions to lure
tourists down from the high fells and lakes to the north: as the birthplace of Stan Laurel
it boasts an endearingly eccentric Laurel and Hardy Museum in King Street; visitors
are also welcomed at the modern Cumbria Crystal glassworks in Lightburn Road.

GRANGE-OVER-SANDS

Sedately elegant, the nineteenth-century seaside resort of Grange-over-Sands
spreads out on a gentle wooded hillside overlooking the vast sands of Morecambe Bay.
Since medieval times at least, Grange has been at one end of the main route for
crossing the sands at low tide, and there is still an official guide to steer small parties
of walkers amongst the swirling channels to Bolton-le-Sands on the south-
eastern side. Grange grew to prominence, however, when the Furness Railway arrived
here in 1857, bringing with it scores of holidaymakers from Lancashire's
industrial towns. On a stretch of coastline known optimistically as the 'Cumbrian
Riviera' because of its gentle (or gentler) climate, it is something of a retirement
town nowadays. It still has some of the air of a small resort, with an attractive mile-
long promenade, a swimming pool – whose startling blue rather throws into
the shade the muddy brown of the real coastline surrounding it – ornamental gardens,
tennis and bowls. From Hampsfield Fell above the town one can see the Isle of
Man on a clear day.

ARNSIDE

*Although it is outside the National Park, the countryside round Arnside and its
neighbour, Silverdale, has been designated an Area of Outstanding Natural Beauty
and it is chiefly the lovely surroundings that draw visitors to this small seaside
resort on the Kent Estuary. The limestone outcrop of Arnside Knott, at the top right of
the picture, provides spectacular views of Morecambe Bay and the southern Lakeland fells.*

PIEL CASTLE

The imposing castle on Piel Island is perfectly sited for guarding the important
harbour of Barrow-in-Furness: the island lies between the twin jaws of Walney Island
to the south and Roa Island to the north. The castle, whose ruins date from
1327, belonged to the monks of nearby Furness Abbey and was probably used as a
fortified warehouse to keep cargoes safe from pirates.

PIEL ISLAND

*Teardrop-shaped Piel Island makes an attractive composition when seen from
above with Walney Island beyond. As well as the castle, nowadays there is also a pub
to refresh visitors who come over on the ferry from Roa Island, and the
eighteenth-century ships' pilots' houses are used as holiday homes by
modern-day sailors.*

ROA ISLAND

Roa Island, just south of Barrow-in-Furness, was first named by Norse settlers
to the region. It remained an island until the 1840s when a railway embankment was
built to transport passengers to and from the pier, from where a steamship
service operated between Barrow and Belfast. This pier was replaced by a more
convenient deep-water berth in Barrow Docks in the 1880s.

HAWS POINT, WALNEY ISLAND

Long, thin Walney Island shelters Barrow-in-Furness from the Irish Sea and
provides a welcome contrast to the bleakness of the industrial coastline. There is a
Nature Reserve here with colonies of gulls and eider ducks and, on the west
coast, a vast beach twelve miles long. The picture shows Haws Point in the south of
the island, with North East Point in the foreground.

BARROW-IN-FURNESS

With its huge harbour formed to the south by *Walney Island*, Barrow grew up
as an industrial port in the nineteenth century on the back of the south Cumbrian iron
industry. Although hardly beautiful, it is well planned and has a splendid
Gothic town hall (which can be seen near the centre of the picture) dating to 1887.
With a workforce of 12,000, Vickers shipbuilders is the town's major employer.

FURNESS ABBEY

Built of glowing pink local sandstone, the beautiful ruins of Furness Abbey
spread out in a lovely wooded valley just north of Barrow-in-Furness. Founded in 1127
as a Savigniac house, it became Cistercian in 1147 and was soon the order's
second richest abbey in England, with vast estates in Cumbria including large parts of
the Lake District where the monks developed sheep farming on an organised basis.

89

MILLOM

The industrial town of Millom is scarcely a beautiful place but its situation
beside the Duddon estuary, with dramatic fells close by to both north and east, is
spectacular. It grew up in the second half of the nineteenth century after the discovery here
of exceptionally rich seams of iron ore; the huge Hodbarrow Mines, which finally closed in
1968, are just to the south of the town, protected by a mile-long sea wall.

BROUGHTON-IN-FURNESS

Broughton-in-Furness, at the head of the Duddon estuary, is a small town –
hardly more than a village – of considerable sleepy charm. Most of the buildings in the
market square date to the eighteenth century; the town hall on one side has
taken on a new lease of life as the Lakeland Motorcycle Museum. The obelisk in the
centre was added in 1810 to commemorate the golden jubilee of George III.

DEVOKE WATER

On lonely Birker Fell, south of Eskdale, is Devoke Water, the largest stretch of
water in the Lake District to be officially regarded as a tarn. These windswept hills are
not far from the coast where Stone Age sites have been discovered and it seems
they too were well known to early man – at the far end of the lake and beyond are
numerous Bronze Age burial mounds, cairns, and traces of settlement.

CONISTON WATER

Seen here from near its northern end, Coniston Water is nearly 5½ miles long
and very straight: it was this that attracted the famous Sir Malcolm Campbell and
later his son Donald to use it in their attempts on the world water speed record.
On 4th January 1967 Donald was tragically killed here while trying to reach
300 mph; his body was never found.

THE OLD MAN OF CONISTON

*The great ridge of the Coniston group is a spectacular sight with its coating of
snow. The sharply defined horseshoe, seen to the left of the reservoir, Seathwaite Tarn,
has as its left side the comfortable summit of Old Man and, as its right, the
great rock face of Dow Crag. There is a glorious view from above this fearsome
precipice of little Goat's Water, nearly a thousand feet below.*

THE OLD MAN OF CONISTON

'Not Man's hills but all for themselves the sky and the clouds.' Dorothy
Wordsworth's sentiments about the Coniston Fells can still be shared today, a tribute
to the dignity of the Old Man, whose mine-scarred summit (in the foreground
as we look north) is now a favourite objective for Lakeland visitors. Goat's Water, Low
Water and Levers Water are seen from left to right, and Swirl How ahead.

THE OLD MAN OF CONISTON

*Although much climbed – the walk to reach its 2,635 ft summit takes about two
hours from Coniston village – the Old Man of Coniston is not a very beautiful
mountain. The Old Man has had a hard working life, and his flanks are
scarred and lined by the remains of both copper mining and slate quarrying. This view
shows Levers Water and, beyond it, just under the peak of the Old Man, Low Water.*

HIGH YEWDALE

Bleak, windswept Wetherlam towers over High Yewdale; guide books warn of
the mountain's disused mine shafts. To the right is Holm Fell and, beside the neat row
of conifers in the centre, High Yewdale Farm – one of the many farms donated
by Mrs William Heelis (Beatrix Potter) to the National Trust. Beautiful Tarn Hows is
just out of view to the near right.

WALLS CASTLE

This is not a castle at all but the extraordinarily well-preserved shell of a
Roman bath house, all that is left of the fort of Glannaventa which served as a naval
base for north-west England. The walls are ten feet high, clearly showing the
room divisions and doorways. Roman bath houses usually consisted of a frigidarium,
a tepidarium, and a caldarium, sometimes with a sauna-type laconicum too.

MUNCASTER CASTLE

In pink local granite, Muncaster Castle, ancient seat of the Pennington family,
is based on a pele tower dating to 1325 which was added to in the fifteenth and
sixteenth centuries and remodelled in Victorian times. In the seventeenth
century such was the fame of the castle's jester, Thomas Skelton, that the words 'tom
fool' and 'tomfoolery' became part of our language.

In beautifully landscaped parkland beside the Esk, a mile from its estuary at
Ravenglass, the castle has one of the loveliest sites of any Lakeland stately home. The
Terrace Walk – its box and yew hedge can be seen in the centre foreground –
is famous for its rhododendrons and azaleas. Ruskin described the view looking north-
east to Scafell from here as 'the finest in England'.

RAVENGLASS

It is hard to believe today that the little coastal village of Ravenglass was once
an important Roman port, the supply base for the conquest of north-west England:
from here a road led via Mediobogdum on the Hardknott Pass to Galava at
Ambleside. In medieval times it was again important as a port for trade with Ireland,
and was a thriving market town.

LOWER ESKDALE

Eskdale is a valley of subtle contrasts, providing a refreshing change in scenery
from the more dramatic valleys to the east. In its lower reaches, the Esk meanders
prettily amidst green meadows beside Muncaster Fell before broadening into a
mass of mudflats and intricate tidal channels at its confluence with the Mite and Irt,
at Ravenglass, for its final short passage to the sea.

RAVENGLASS AND ESKDALE RAILWAY

This is the Ravenglass terminus of one of the most popular methods of visiting
Eskdale – the narrow-gauge Ravenglass and Eskdale Railway, or 'La'al Ratty' to use
the local term of endearment. A 40-minute, seven-mile trip by open and saloon
coaches takes you through glorious scenery to the eastern terminus at Dalegarth.
Originally built in 1875 to carry iron ore, it is now a successful tourist attraction.

OUTWARD BOUND CENTRE, ESKDALE GREEN

*The village of Eskdale Green is home to one of two Lake District centres
belonging to the Outward Bound Trust. Housed in a Victorian mansion overlooking a
lake, Outward Bound Eskdale, as it is known, can accommodate 120 participants on the
Trust's courses where the intrepidly minded learn such sports as rock-climbing, canoeing
and orienteering. Beyond the centre is remote Miterdale with its dense covering of forest.*

ESKDALE

The lovely valley of the Esk is green and wooded in its middle reaches, its
gentleness contrasting with the soaring heights at the head of the valley in the
distance: Scafell can be seen on the horizon to the left. In the left foreground is
the Ravenglass and Eskdale Railway which joins the dale from Miterdale and goes up
as far as Dalegarth Station.

BLEA TARN

*As well as sixteen lakes, the Lake District has innumerable small tarns – no
less than 463 were counted by the famous 'tarn baggers' of Grasmere, who swam in
every one of them in the 1950s. Several of the tarns are named Blea Tarn – the
name means dark blue. The one shown here fills a hollow on the fellside just west of
Boot in Eskdale.*

BLEA TARN

Photographed as the plane flies lower over its banks, Blea Tarn has unexpected
beauty. Its sloping shore, clad with bracken – that ever-encroaching scourge of the
Lakeland farmer – in its restful summer colours gives way to waters that are at
first dark and forbidding but which break into a thousand sparkling ripples as the sun
comes out overhead.

BIRKER FORCE, ESKDALE

Subtly varied shades of green moorland contrast prettily with the shining water
of a mountain stream before, at Birker Force, it plummets towards Eskdale far below.
Not surprisingly, the Lake District abounds in fine waterfalls: the Lodore Falls,
Scale Force and Stanley Force are just some of the better known. Particularly admired
during the nineteenth century for their picturesque qualities, they drew many Victorian walkers.

HARDKNOTT ROMAN FORT

Brilliantly positioned on the shoulder of Hardknott Fell is the fort of
Mediobogdum, one of the country's most remarkable Roman relics. Built in Hadrian's
reign (AD 117-38) it was virtually impregnable owing to the surrounding
crags. The internal plan is similar to Galava's although in addition, just outside the
walls, are the remains of a three-roomed bath house.

HARDKNOTT PASS

Hardknott Pass is the dramatic climax of a Roman road that once stretched
from the sea port of Glannaventa (Ravenglass) to Galava (Ambleside). After passing
through Eskdale, the route climbed up over Hardknott, down into the Duddon
Valley, across Wrynose Pass and into Little Langdale. The modern motorist will
occasionally glimpse the faint grassy track tramped by the Roman cohorts.

BOOT

*A cluster of stone and whitewashed cottages around the Woolpack Inn, the
quaintly named hamlet of Boot lies half-way along sparsely populated Eskdale. Once a
centre for iron ore and copper mining, Boot is visited today for its sixteenth-
century corn mill (beyond the packhorse bridge on the left of the picture), which has
now been restored and opened to the public.*

PIKE OF BLISCO

Wainwright urges an approach to Crinkle Crags via the 'rocky top of Pike o'
Blisco', describing it as a pleasant and colourful place. Pike of Blisco is distinctive for
its symmetry, and the views from its summit provide a well-deserved reward for
walkers: here it is seen from the East with Crinkle Crags beyond, Crinkle Gill below,
Bowfell to the right and Scafell Pike in the background.

THE LANGDALE PIKES

Craggy, once volcanic, Wordsworth's 'five solemn pikes of Langdale' are recognised and revered not only by fell-walkers and rock-climbers but by the uninitiated who appreciate their majestic profile from the far distance. Pike of Stickle is in the foreground, Loft Crag to its right, the crowning summit Harrison Stickle beyond with Thorn Crag between, and Pavey Ark to the left.

PIKE OF STICKLE

These walkers are on the thimble-shaped summit of Pike of Stickle (2323 feet).
As Wainwright says, there is little scope for exploration here, with the ground falling
away in precipices on both sides. However, the views are magnificent – to the
next goal, Loft Crag, to proud Harrison Stickle, and out to the green pastures of Great
Langdale beyond.

The discovery in 1947 of an axe-head in this wide scree gully was the first clue
that an industry was based here in Neolithic times for the manufacture of stone axes
from a finely-grained volcanic ash called porcellenite. The unearthing of further
examples and chipping sites has established Langdale as the most significant site of this
kind in the country.

GREAT GABLE

Great Gable's famous and stately silhouette crowns the heads of both Wasdale
and Ennerdale. The easiest way up is via the path (to the left) known as Moses Trod,
which is named after an illicit whisky maker who allegedly had his still on the
mountain. Shown here are, to the left, wooded Ennerdale and, directly ahead,
Haystacks from where the land drops away to the Buttermere valley.

CRINKLE CRAGS

*Anyone exploring the jagged sky-line of Crinkle Crags will understand why
they were so named by the first settlers (although the Old Norse word kringla,
meaning a circle, may also have contributed). There are five summits, and to
walk from the first to the last is, according to Wainwright, 'an exciting adventure'.
The Crags are seen here from the south with the twinned Bowfell Links ahead.*

GREAT GABLE

*Great Gable impressed Wordsworth as 'the loftiest, a distinct and huge form'
and it certainly makes a stirring sight, captured here by the camera as the aeroplane
hovers almost due west of its summit. On the right are the craggy Great Napes
and, falling away beneath, one of the flat faces that give the mountain the appearance
of a gigantic pyramid when viewed from Wasdale.*

WASTWATER

The Lake District's deepest lake – Wastwater at 258 feet – is fittingly
surrounded by some of the area's most impressive scenery. On the right are the famous
Screes, which plunge to the lake floor from the crags of Illgill Head, making a
total drop of almost 2000 feet; at the far end of the lake in the centre is the unmistakable
pyramidal shape of Great Gable, now used as the National Park's official logo.

WASDALE, FROM KIRK FELL

To stand between Great Gable's western flank and Kirk Fell's eastern one is to
gain a breathtaking view south-west down into the valley of Wasdale. From Beck
Head (the name also given to the small tarn in the foreground), Gable Beck
flows down to join Lingmell Beck which snakes all the way to Wastwater (just visible
straight ahead, behind the clouds). The tarn gleaming in the distance is Burnmoor.

117

WASDALE HEAD

Surrounded by fells of awe-inspiring grandeur – the Scafells, Great Gable and
Pillar – the tiny village of Wasdale Head was the cradle of Lakeland rock-climbing.
From the early 1880s the hotel here became a magnet for aspiring mountaineers who came
from all over the country to challenge such climbs as Pillar Rock and Napes Needle.
It has retained its splendid sense of isolation and remains the premier fell-walking centre.

SCAFELL AREA

Blanketing the cultivated valley bottoms so that only the high peaks remain,
the clouds give Lakeland's highest fells a secretive, almost primeval air. A massive
display of volcanic violence created the rocks of this central area, known as the
Borrowdale Volcanics, about 450 million years ago; later catastrophic earth
movements pushed them up into an elongated dome to form the Lake District's core.

SCAFELL PIKE

At 3206 feet Scafell Pike is the highest mountain in England. A spectacular,
barren hill with sharply etched glacial corries, it has three principal summits: Broad
Crag (3054 ft), Ill Crag (3040 ft) and Scafell Pike itself. In the left-hand
picture Scafell Pike is on the left, descending to the Mickledore Gap; to the right is the
slightly lower summit of Scafell (3162 ft) buttressed by the formidable bastion
of Scafell Crag. Scafell Pike attracts thousands of walkers and climbers every year on
five main routes to the summit: from Wasdale Head, Eskdale, Great Langdale
and two from Borrowdale. In the right hand picture we can see Scafell's gradual
southern slopes. Greencove Wyke is in the foreground, Mickledore Gap to the
right and Wastwater behind with long bulk of Yewbarrow rising up from its shores.

HAYSTACKS LOOKING TOWARDS BUTTERMERE

In spite of its small stature – at only 1,900 feet it is dwarfed by neighbouring
Pillar and Great Gable – Haystacks, with its abrupt, rugged crags dropping
vertiginously to the Buttermere valley to the north-west, is a vastly impressive
mountain. Its summit, too, is a delight: a glorious profusion of small pools and tarns,
rocky outcrops, tracts of marsh and small screes.

PILLAR

Pillar (2927 ft) is the highest of the three great ridges in the Mosedale Horseshoe.
Early shepherds gave this giant its name, referring as Wordsworth explained, to
'one particular rock, That rises like a column from the vale'. Pillar Rock, its upper
part seen here as we face Pillar's daunting north flank, has been a challenge to
rock-climbers since some locals conquered the awe-inspiring crags in the 1860s.

PILLAR

Looking northwards from near the summit of Pillar, a magnificent panorama
unfolds. The next valley, densely planted, is Ennerdale; then comes the ridge
comprising Red Pike, High Stile and High Crag; then the Buttermere valley –
Crummock Water can just be seen and, to the far left, Loweswater. Rising behind
Crummock Water is the Grasmoor group; in the far distance to the right is Skiddaw.

EGREMONT

The old market town of Egremont stands between the western Lakeland fells
and the coastal plain at a crossing point of the River Ehen. Its greatest claim to fame is
the annual Crab Fair, held in September, a traditional country fair probably
originally connected with crab apples rather than seafood. It includes a peculiar
competition where contestants vie to pull the ugliest face while wearing a horse collar.

EGREMONT CASTLE

Founded probably by William de Meschines in c.1120, Egremont's castle, a
proud red sandstone fortress that was 150 years in the building, was one of the
Norman chain that ringed the high ground of the Lake District. It had a
turbulent history, being besieged by Robert the Bruce and later by the feared and hated
'Black' Douglas, but has been ruinous since the sixteenth century.

ST BEES

The two finest buildings in St Bees, separated from the main part of the village
by the railway, are the school, founded in 1538, with its original buildings still
standing in the three-sided courtyard, and the handsome priory church, facing
it. It seems likely there was a church here from at least the tenth century, and a
Benedictine community from York established the priory between 1121 and 1138.

ST BEES HEAD

The pink cliffs of St Bees Head, surmounted by a neat patchwork of fields, form
the westernmost point of Lakeland; a cliff-top walk from Whitehaven to St Bees
provides views of the Isle of Man. A favourite with geologists, this glowing
sandstone coastline was formed 200 million years ago in the Permian period. The cliffs
house the country's only colony of black guillemots and there is an RSPB
Nature Reserve with look-out points. It seems that the first Cumbrians inhabited St
Bees and other coastal regions in Mesolithic times, the lack of forestation and
the supply of flint, fish and wild fowl providing the means of support they needed. We
are looking north to Saltom Bay with the buildings of Whitehaven just visible
in the distance.

ENNERDALE WATER

Ennerdale Water's isolated location on the western side of the Lake District, its
reservoir status and the fact that no road circles the lake have kept this a peaceful spot,
even in high summer. Conservationists, too, have played their part in preserving
its beauty: in the nineteenth century a proposal to build a railway along Ennerdale
was defeated, and in 1978 a major new reservoir scheme here was thrown out.

ENNERDALE

Made dark and austere by its armies of conifers, Ennerdale was the product of
early Forestry Commission planting policy in the 1930s. The regimented lines of trees
aroused furious local criticism and led to an agreement by the Forestry
Commission not to undertake any new planting in central Lakeland. Since the early
1980s the Commission has been working to produce a more natural-looking forest.

WHITEHAVEN

Whitehaven's neat gridiron layout and complex series of harbour walls and
piers give it a workmanlike appearance. Planned specifically as an industrial town
when coal was discovered on this part of the coast, it became at one time
England's third port (after London and Liverpool). The pits have long been closed,
though, and the town's major employer is now British Nuclear Fuels at Sellafield.

ENNERDALE BRIDGE

The River Ehen twists and turns from Ennerdale Water out to the sea; at its
highest crossing, and on the western boundary of the National Park, is the village of
Ennerdale Bridge. A visit to a former chapel on the site of the present Church of
St Mary was the inspiration for Wordsworth's poem 'The Brothers'. The village is a
good starting point for exploration of the Ennerdale Valley.

BUTTERMERE

Seen here from near the summit of Haystacks, little Buttermere occupies an
idyllic site, hemmed in on either side by imposing fells: High Crag and High Stile to
the west (they can be seen on the left), Buttermere Fell to the east, and, to
contrast with this, lush green meadows filling the valley floor at either end. Between
Buttermere and Crummock Water beyond is tiny Buttermere village.

BUTTERMERE VALLEY

Only a few flat green fields separate Crummock Water (to the right) from
Buttermere and it is easy to see that the two were once a single lake. The alluvial
plain which divides them was formed from debris washed down by mountain
streams, after the last Ice Age brought powerful erosive forces to bear on the surface
rocks. In the foreground is the abrupt rocky hump of Rannerdale Knotts.

SLATE QUARRY, HONISTER PASS

The top of Honister Pass was until recently the site of one of Lakeland's
industrial success stories, the Buttermere and Westmorland Green Slate Company.
Slate is first recorded as being quarried here in 1643 and in the eighteenth
century the industry expanded greatly; the prized green slate was split and polished for
a multitude of uses from roofing and paving to cladding buildings and ornaments.

CRUMMOCK WATER

The most graceful, and the highest, of the steep fells which line the shores of
Crummock Water is pyramidal Grasmoor, seen here on the left. Crummock Water
shares its valley with Buttermere, which can just be seen beyond; Crummock
Water, two and a half miles long, is the larger of the twins. In the foreground, the
River Cocker can be seen winding through the trees on its way north to Cockermouth.

GRANGE

Grange, in the lower part of the valley, is one of Borrowdale's prettiest villages.
Its graceful double-arched bridge, built in 1675, leads over the Derwent to an
attractive huddle of stone cottages on the western side. The village's name refers
to its history as an outlying grange or abbey farm – it was acquired by the monks of
powerful Furness Abbey in 1209.

CASTLE CRAG, BORROWDALE

Borrowdale takes its name from the Scandinavian borgardalr meaning 'the
valley of the fort'. The remains of this fort can be traced on the top of the impressive
outcrop of Castle Crag, which occupies a superb defensive position in a narrow
rocky gorge. The Romans arrived in the Lake District in AD 90; forts such as this may
have been centres of British resistance to the invaders.

TAYLORGILL FORCE

One of Lakeland's most spectacular waterfalls, Taylorgill Force cascades in two
delicate ribbons between the scree slopes of Base Brown and gentler Seathwaite Fell. Its
waters come from Styhead Tarn at the foot of Great Gable and from several mountain
streams; since lucky Seathwaite, nearby, is the wettest place in Britain – it records over
120 inches of rain annually – Taylorgill is a fine sight at most times of year.

RIVER DERWENT

After its exit from the northern end of Bassenthwaite Lake, the River Derwent
carves a peaceful meandering route for itself through gentle agricultural countryside on
its way to the sea at Workington. This is the far north-western corner of the
Lake District National Park – the boundary comes just before the river reaches
Cockermouth in the distance to the left.

ROSTHWAITE

South of the Jaws of Borrowdale is some of the richest pasture in the Lake
District. Set amidst it, between the Stonethwaite Beck (to the right) and the River
Derwent (left), and backed by wooded hillsides is Rosthwaite, the largest of four
hamlets in the upper Borrowdale valley. Surrounding it the network of dry stone walls
makes an elegant patchwork in the autumn sunlight.

VIEW FROM NEAR GREAT END LOOKING NORTH-WEST

Seen in their autumn colouring, when the bracken blends with the bare, rocky
fell tops to produce a burnt, almost parched appearance, the central mountains of the
Cumbrian chain have a stark beauty very different from that of summer. In the
centre of the picture is Great End, with little Sprinkling Tarn below to its right; beyond
is Great Gable and, in the distance, Buttermere and Crummock Water.

WATENDLATH

Just to the south-east of Derwent Water is a classic example of a distinctive
glacial feature – the hanging valley of Watendlath. This little side valley was left
much higher than the main neighbouring valley, Borrowdale, after the latter
was deepened by the action of a glacier during the last Ice Age. As a result, the
Watendlath Beck has to drop sharply when it reaches the end of the side valley
on the shores of Derwent Water: the waterfall thus created is the famous Lodore Falls.

A tiny, secret-looking hamlet hidden in a high valley beside a dark tarn,
Watendlath was the setting for Judith Paris, one of the novels in Sir Hugh
Walpole's Rogue Herries chronicles. Unfortunately quite a few tourists have
discovered its charms and the narrow valley road is congested in summer. Some also
come for the fish: the tarn is well stocked with brown and rainbow trout.

BORROWDALE

In many ways, Borrowdale is the quintessential Lake District valley: its lush
pastures, romantic rocky crags, fine broadleaved woodlands and backdrop of towering
fells have made it a favourite with visitors since the early nineteenth century. Shown here
is the rocky gorge known as the 'Jaws' of Borrowdale in the foreground, with the lower
part of the valley, where the River Derwent enters Derwent Water, beyond.

DERWENT WATER FROM SKIDDAW

From above Longside Edge on Skiddaw looking south, the view is spectacular.
Ahead lies the attractive town of Keswick and blue Derwent Water, with Borrowdale
beyond. In the distance to the left, in the shadow of Helvellyn, is Thirlmere
while to the right, topped with clouds, are some of the giants of central Lakeland –
Bowfell, Great End and Scafell Pike.

DERWENT WATER

It is easy to see why Derwent Water, with its unusual, almost oval shape, its
towering backdrop of ancient Skiddaw and its scattering of inviting-looking small
islands has become known as 'Queen of the Lakes'. St Herbert's Island is
closest to the camera here; in addition to those seen in the picture Derwent Water
occasionally has a curious 'extra' floating island composed of tangled vegetation.